MAYER SMITH

Disguised in Poverty,
Loved in Truth

Copyright © 2025 by Mayer Smith

All rights reserved. No part of this publication may be reproduced, stored or transmitted in any form or by any means, electronic, mechanical, photocopying, recording, scanning, or otherwise without written permission from the publisher. It is illegal to copy this book, post it to a website, or distribute it by any other means without permission.

This novel is entirely a work of fiction. The names, characters and incidents portrayed in it are the work of the author's imagination. Any resemblance to actual persons, living or dead, events or localities is entirely coincidental.

Mayer Smith asserts the moral right to be identified as the author of this work.

Mayer Smith has no responsibility for the persistence or accuracy of URLs for external or third-party Internet Websites referred to in this publication and does not guarantee that any content on such Websites is, or will remain, accurate or appropriate.

Designations used by companies to distinguish their products are often claimed as trademarks. All brand names and product names used in this book and on its cover are trade names, service marks, trademarks and registered trademarks of their respective owners. The publishers and the book are not associated with any product or vendor mentioned in this book. None of the companies referenced within the book have endorsed the book.

First edition

*This book was professionally typeset on Reedsy.
Find out more at reedsy.com*

Contents

1	The Secretive Billionaire	1
2	The Mysterious Woman	8
3	A Different Kind of Man	15
4	Unlikely Bonds	21
5	A Moment of Weakness	28
6	The Tipping Point	35
7	The Shadows of the Past	41
8	Breaking Point	48
9	Secrets Exposed	55
10	The Cost of Truth	62
11	The Struggle for Redemption	69
12	A Test of Faith	77
13	The Final Choice	84
14	The Heart's Desire	91
15	A Love Rekindled	97

One

The Secretive Billionaire

It was a quiet evening in New York City, the kind that made you feel like the world outside had slipped into another dimension. The lights of the skyscrapers glimmered like distant stars, and the streets below were filled with the usual chaos: honking horns, hurried footsteps, and the low hum of the city that never slept. But within the walls of one particular penthouse, high above the frenzy, Alexander Greyson sat in silence.

The lavish apartment, decorated in sleek, modern furniture and expensive art, seemed almost empty. Not because there was a lack of belongings, but because there was an absence of warmth—a stark contrast to the wealth and power it represented. Alexander, the heir to one of the largest tech empires in the world, stood in front of a floor-to-ceiling window that overlooked the glowing skyline. His piercing blue eyes gazed out, but they were not focused on the view. His mind was elsewhere, lost in thoughts he had been running from for months.

He had it all: a multi-billion-dollar empire, a fleet of luxury cars, private jets, and every material possession he could ever want. Yet, something was missing. No matter how much he had, he felt as if he was living in a gilded cage—a prisoner to his own success. The faceless people who smiled at him, the endless parties filled with shallow conversations, and the superficial relationships that surrounded him—all of it had begun to feel suffocating. Alexander craved something real. Something genuine. Something that didn't come with an ulterior motive.

His phone buzzed on the marble countertop, snapping him from his reverie. He glanced down, seeing a message from his assistant, Olivia.

"Your meeting with the board is in an hour. Shall I prepare the car?"

He stared at the message for a long moment before typing a brief response.

"Cancel the meeting. I'm not interested."

He paused, letting the weight of his words sink in. He wasn't interested. He didn't care about the business empire he had inherited. He didn't care about the board members or their constant demands. What he cared about now was finding something that had eluded him for years—real love.

Love. It was a concept he had long ago dismissed as an illusion, a fairy tale reserved for the naive. He had been in relationships before, but they had always ended in disappointment. Women who pretended to care, only to reveal they were more interested in his money and status than the man behind the fortune. It wasn't love. It was a transaction. A game.

But he didn't want a game anymore. He wanted truth. He wanted to feel what it was like to be loved for who he was, not what he could provide. So, after months of agonizing over the idea, he had come to a decision that would alter the course of his life forever.

He would disappear.

Not just from the city, but from his entire world.

Alexander Greyson, billionaire and heir to a tech empire, would erase every trace of his wealth and live as a common man. For once, he would live without the shadow of his family's fortune hanging over him. And, more importantly, he would test the sincerity of love.

He didn't know where this idea had come from or what exactly he hoped to find, but it was the only thing that had sparked a flicker of hope within him. He had to try. He had to know if love was truly possible, or if it was always going to be tainted by greed and ambition.

The next morning, Alexander was no longer Alexander Greyson.

He had already secured a fake identity—Alex Garrett. A man with no past, no connections, and no wealth to speak of. He sold off his penthouse and most of his assets, leaving only a modest bank account. The luxury cars and private jets were gone, replaced by a secondhand car and a cheap apartment in a quiet corner of a small town.

The town was nothing like the bustling city he had grown accustomed to. There were no towering skyscrapers or expensive restaurants. The streets were lined with simple houses, and the air was thick with the scent of fresh bread from the local bakery. It was peaceful, almost too peaceful for someone who had been at the center of so much power and chaos.

But this was exactly what Alexander needed. He needed to strip away everything that had defined him and start fresh. He needed to immerse himself in a world where no one knew him, where his past didn't matter. And he needed to find someone who could love him for who he was—not for his fortune, his title, or his social standing.

It was a bold plan, but one that filled him with both excitement and trepidation. He had no idea how long he could keep up the ruse, or how people would react when they found out the truth. But for the first time in a long while, Alexander felt something he hadn't felt in years—an inkling of hope.

The town was small, and its residents kept to themselves. Yet, there was a certain charm to the simplicity of it all. He spent his days walking through the streets, getting to know the locals. The bakery owners, the grocery store clerk, the postman—he learned their names, their stories, and their dreams. And yet, despite the comfort of the town, there was still a lingering emptiness.

And then, he saw her.

It was a chance encounter, one that seemed almost fated. She was walking along the street, carrying a basket of groceries in her hands. She had a simple elegance about her, with long brown hair that cascaded over her shoulders and eyes that seemed to hold a quiet strength. She was different from the women he had known in the city—there was no pretension, no calculated charm. She wasn't wearing expensive clothes or a fake smile. She was simply… real.

He didn't know why, but he found himself following her.

She stopped at the small café at the corner of the street, and for a moment, Alexander hesitated. He wasn't sure if he should approach her. After all, what would he say? He was just "Alex" now. A regular guy. But something about her drew him in. It was as if fate had given him this moment, this opportunity to test his plan, to see if love could truly be found in a world where money had no place.

Without thinking, he walked up to the café, sat at an empty table, and waited. His heart raced, unsure of what to expect.

And then, she entered the café.

As she stepped inside, she scanned the room, her gaze briefly meeting his. She gave him a polite smile, but there was something in her eyes—a wariness, as if she could sense there was something more to him than met the eye.

He took a deep breath and raised his hand slightly, as if offering a silent greeting.

She hesitated for a moment, then walked toward him.

"Is this seat taken?" she asked softly, her voice warm yet cautious.

"No, it's not," he replied, his voice steadier than he felt.

She sat down, placing her basket on the table. There was a long pause before either of them spoke again.

"I don't think I've seen you around here before," she said, her eyes studying him with mild curiosity.

"I just moved here," he replied, offering a small smile. "I'm Alex."

"Emily," she said, extending her hand.

As their hands met, something shifted between them—something that neither of them could explain. It was subtle, but undeniable. A spark, a connection, a promise that neither of them had expected.

And in that moment, Alexander Greyson, or rather Alex Garrett, knew that his journey had just begun. The woman before him, with her simplicity and sincerity, was unlike anyone he had ever met. And yet, he knew that this was the test he had been waiting for. Could someone love him for who he truly was, or would he always be a man defined by his wealth?

The game had begun.

But for the first time in a long while, Alexander wasn't sure if he was ready for the stakes.

Two

The Mysterious Woman

The morning after their chance encounter, Alex Garrett stood at the window of his small apartment, gazing out over the sleepy town. The sun had only just risen, casting a soft orange glow over the horizon. The town was quiet, still—a stark contrast to the hustle and bustle of New York City. And yet, despite the tranquility of the surroundings, his mind raced with thoughts of Emily.

He couldn't stop thinking about her—about the way her eyes had met his, about the subtle tension that had hung in the air when they shook hands. Something about her intrigued him, something he couldn't quite put his finger on. It wasn't just the way she looked or the quiet grace she carried herself with. It was something deeper—something in the way she had carried herself, as if she didn't quite belong in this small town, yet was at home in it all the same.

The Mysterious Woman

Her name was Emily Clarke, and that was all Alex knew about her. He hadn't asked too many questions, didn't want to seem too eager or too intrusive. He had to remind himself that he was here for a reason, and that reason wasn't to fall into another meaningless relationship. No, he was here to test something far more important—the sincerity of love, and whether it could survive in a world that had always been tainted by wealth and power.

But as he thought about her, he realized that Emily was unlike anyone he had ever met. There was an authenticity to her, a raw honesty that made him feel like he could be himself—something he hadn't felt in years. He didn't have to pretend, didn't have to hide behind a façade of success. For the first time in a long while, he felt as if he could breathe.

But the more he thought about her, the more he wondered what it was that she saw in him. He wasn't anyone special. At least, not in the way that people in his old world would define it. He had no money, no status, no grand title to flaunt. He was just Alex, a simple man trying to make his way through life.

He needed to see her again. And so, he made up his mind.

That afternoon, Alex found himself walking through the quiet streets of the town, his heart pounding in his chest. He didn't have a plan, didn't know what he was going to say, but something told him he had to see her. He had to know more about her. What made her tick? What was her story? Could he even trust his own feelings at this point?

The café was only a few blocks from his apartment, nestled between an old bookstore and a small florist shop. As he approached, he noticed Emily sitting at one of the outdoor tables, her back to him. She was sipping a cup of coffee, staring out at the street, her expression unreadable. He hesitated for a moment, unsure of whether to approach. He didn't want to seem too forward, too eager.

But something pushed him forward. He took a deep breath, walked toward her, and gently tapped the back of her chair.

"Mind if I join you?" he asked, his voice softer than usual, almost tentative.

Emily looked up, her eyes locking with his. There was a flicker of surprise, but it quickly faded into something more neutral. She glanced at the empty chair across from her, then back at him.

"Sure, take a seat," she replied, her tone polite but guarded.

Alex sat down, the air between them thick with unspoken words. They both seemed to be waiting for the other to speak, but neither knew where to start. It was as if a veil of uncertainty hung over them, one that neither of them could seem to lift.

"Is it always this quiet here?" Alex finally asked, his voice breaking the silence.

Emily looked around, her gaze softening as she took in the town around them. "It can be," she said with a slight smile. "It's nice, though. I like it that way."

Alex nodded, but his mind wasn't on the town. He was focused entirely on her. There was something about her that made him feel as if he could tell her anything, as if she would understand. But at the same time, there was a wall around her, something that made it clear she wasn't an open book. She held her secrets close, and he couldn't help but wonder what those secrets were.

"So, what brings you to this town?" Emily asked after a long pause, her voice breaking through his thoughts.

Alex hesitated, choosing his words carefully. He wasn't used to explaining himself to anyone. Not like this, anyway. "I needed a change of pace," he said, offering a small shrug. "A fresh start, I guess."

Emily studied him for a moment, her eyes narrowing slightly, as if weighing his words. "A fresh start?" she echoed. "From what?"

Alex froze for a split second, his heart skipping a beat. There it was—the question he had been dreading. The one question he wasn't sure he was ready to answer. He could lie, of course. He could make up some story about running away from a failed business venture, or about needing to escape a toxic relationship. But something about the way Emily looked at him made it impossible to lie.

He could see it in her eyes—the quiet challenge, the subtle probing. She wasn't just making small talk. She was trying to figure him out, to understand who he really was.

"I... I guess you could say I was running from myself," he finally admitted, the words slipping out before he could stop them. "From the life I had built. It wasn't... it wasn't fulfilling."

Emily raised an eyebrow, clearly intrigued, but she didn't press further. Instead, she offered him a soft smile, as if she understood more than she let on. "I get that," she said quietly. "Sometimes we need to leave things behind to find what we're really looking for."

Alex didn't know if she was referring to herself, or if she was just offering him an understanding of his own struggles. Either way, her words hit a nerve, and he felt an unexpected surge of gratitude.

They sat in silence for a moment, the weight of their shared understanding hanging between them. It was strange, this connection they had. It was as if they had both been carrying burdens they couldn't share with anyone else—until now.

"So, tell me more about you, Alex," Emily said, breaking the silence. "What's your story? Who are you really?"

It was a simple question, but it carried more weight than she likely realized. Who was he, really? What was he doing here? The man she saw sitting across from her was just a shadow of the life he had once known. The man she saw was someone he had created—a new identity, a new beginning. But the real question was, could he keep up the lie?

The Mysterious Woman

He stared at her for a moment, trying to gauge whether she was truly interested, or if she was just passing the time. But her eyes were sincere, and for reasons he couldn't explain, he felt the urge to tell her the truth. Or at least part of it.

"I guess I'm still trying to figure that out," he said quietly. "But I think I'm getting closer."

Emily seemed to consider this for a moment, her gaze softening. "We all are," she said finally. "None of us have all the answers. Not really."

There it was again—the quiet wisdom in her words. Emily was a puzzle, and he was determined to solve it. But as much as he wanted to know her, he couldn't shake the feeling that she, too, was hiding something. Something important.

The conversation drifted after that, the two of them exchanging pleasantries, discussing trivial things—books they liked, favorite movies, the weather. But beneath the surface, there was an unspoken tension, a sense that neither of them was being entirely truthful. And Alex couldn't help but wonder: was Emily hiding something? Or was it him who was wearing the mask?

As the afternoon wore on, Alex found himself both drawn to her and wary of her in equal measure. Emily Clarke was a mystery, and for the first time in a long while, Alex wasn't sure if he was ready to uncover the truth.

But one thing was certain: he couldn't stop thinking about her.

And that alone was enough to make him realize he had already started down a path he wasn't sure he could turn back from.

Three

A Different Kind of Man

The days blurred together as Alex Garrett settled deeper into his new life. The small town, which had once felt unfamiliar and distant, began to feel like a second skin. He woke up early each morning to the sound of birds chirping outside his window and the soft hum of traffic in the distance. He had no pressing meetings to attend, no luxurious events to grace with his presence. For the first time in years, he was truly free.

But as much as he tried to adjust to his new life, there was one constant that kept pulling at him—Emily Clarke. Their conversations, though brief, had left an indelible mark on him. Her words had a way of sticking with him, her gaze seemed to see right through him, and every time she smiled, his heart seemed to beat just a little faster. He couldn't get her out of his head, and the more time he spent with her, the more he questioned his own motives.

He had come to this town with a plan: to live without the trappings of wealth and status, to experience life as an ordinary man, and to find love without the shadow of his fortune hanging over him. But the more he interacted with Emily, the more his resolve began to waver. She was different from any woman he had ever met—different from the shallow socialites he had once been surrounded by, and different from the ambitious women who had only cared for his name and wealth.

Emily didn't seem to care about who he was or what he had. In fact, she didn't seem to care much about anything except the truth. And that truth was what terrified him.

One afternoon, Alex found himself sitting alone in the town's small library, his thoughts once again consumed by Emily. He was supposed to be reading through a few books on local history—something he had promised himself he would do to blend in better—but instead, his mind kept drifting back to the café, to her warm smile, to the way her eyes had locked with his that first day. He had never known anyone quite like her. There was an intelligence in her gaze, an unspoken challenge that made him want to be better, to be someone worthy of her attention.

But how could he ever be worthy of someone like her? He had built a life on deception—on the belief that people would only value him if they knew who he truly was. Now, he was questioning everything he had ever believed. If he couldn't show Emily who he really was, would she still want him? Would she still see him as the man she had met, or would she walk away, disgusted by his lies?

His phone buzzed, breaking his train of thought. The message was from Olivia, his former assistant, still trying to reach him despite his efforts to disconnect from the life he had left behind.

"Alex, the board is pushing for your presence at the next shareholder meeting. They're not going to let you off the hook for long. Let me know what you want to do."

He stared at the message for a long moment, the weight of it hanging over him. The thought of returning to the world he had escaped—of walking back into the glittering, soulless existence he had tried so hard to leave behind—made his stomach turn. But the more he thought about it, the more he realized how much of that life he was still holding onto. Could he truly be free of it?

The sound of footsteps approaching interrupted his thoughts, and Alex looked up to see Emily walking toward him, her arms laden with a stack of books. She was wearing a simple denim jacket and jeans, her hair pulled back into a loose ponytail. She looked effortlessly beautiful, as if she didn't even try to be. Her presence had an almost magnetic quality to it, and for a moment, Alex forgot to breathe.

"Didn't expect to see you here," she said, her voice light, but there was a hint of something else—something deeper—beneath her words. "You're usually at the café."

"I... I thought I'd change things up," Alex said, offering her a nervous smile. "It's a quiet place. Gives me time to think."

Emily placed her books on the table across from him and sat down, her eyes studying him with a quiet curiosity. "You do a lot of thinking, don't you?" she asked, her tone soft but knowing.

Alex hesitated. There was something in the way she looked at him, something that made him feel as though she could see right through him. He wanted to tell her everything, to reveal the truth of who he really was, but the words seemed to catch in his throat.

"I guess you could say that," he replied, forcing himself to sound casual. "I'm not much of a talker, I guess. I prefer to figure things out on my own."

Emily smiled, but there was a flicker of something in her eyes—a trace of skepticism. "I've noticed that about you. You're not exactly the type to open up, are you?"

Alex shifted in his seat, suddenly feeling uncomfortable. He wasn't used to being read so easily. It was always the other way around—he was the one who knew what people were thinking, who could read between the lines and predict their every move. But Emily was different. She didn't play by the same rules.

"I'm just not the sharing type, I suppose," he said, trying to brush it off. "I'm... I'm still adjusting to things here."

"Adjusting?" Emily echoed, her brow furrowing slightly. "To

what?"

"To life," Alex said, his voice softening. He leaned back in his chair, trying to gather his thoughts. "To being someone else. Someone… less complicated."

She regarded him carefully, her gaze never leaving his face. "Less complicated?" she repeated. "You know, I don't think you're as simple as you like to make yourself out to be."

Her words struck him like a punch to the gut. She had no idea. If she only knew the truth about him—the man he really was, the life he had left behind—she would understand just how complicated he really was. But no. He couldn't let her know. Not yet.

"Maybe I'm not," he said, offering her a half-hearted smile. "Maybe I'm just… still figuring it out."

Emily didn't respond immediately. She just sat there, studying him, her fingers tapping lightly on the table. The silence stretched between them, heavy with the weight of unspoken words.

Finally, she spoke again, her voice quiet but firm. "You're hiding something, Alex. I don't know what it is, but I can tell you're not being entirely honest with me. And that's okay. You don't owe me the truth right away. But eventually, you'll have to decide who you want to be. Whether you want to keep running from your past or if you want to face it."

Her words hit him harder than he expected. He wasn't used to people confronting him, especially not so directly. He had spent his whole life building walls, hiding behind them, pretending to be someone he wasn't. And now, Emily—this woman who had somehow wormed her way into his life—was challenging him to confront everything he had buried.

He could feel his resolve slipping, the walls he had so carefully constructed beginning to crack. For the first time in years, Alex found himself questioning his own identity. Who was he? Who did he want to be?

But before he could respond, Emily stood up, gathering her books and preparing to leave. "I'll let you get back to your thinking," she said with a small smile. "But just remember—people can only trust you if you trust them first."

She turned and walked away, leaving Alex alone with his thoughts once again.

He sat there, staring at the empty chair across from him, the echoes of her words still ringing in his ears. She was right, in a way. He couldn't keep hiding forever. Eventually, the truth would come out. And when it did, would Emily still want him? Or would she see him as the fraud he feared he truly was?

Alex Garrett had come to this town to find himself. But now, he was beginning to wonder if he could ever truly escape the man he had been—and whether the life he had left behind would ever truly let him go.

Four

Unlikely Bonds

The weeks that followed were a blur for Alex. He had spent his days slipping further into the role of a man who didn't care about wealth, about status, or about anything that defined the person he used to be. His days were simple—visiting the local bookstore, helping out at the café where Emily worked, and taking long walks through the town. It was a peaceful existence, but underneath the calm, there was a storm brewing. The storm had a name: Emily Clarke.

Every interaction with her seemed to pull him deeper into a world he wasn't sure he was ready for. There was an ease between them that he hadn't experienced before. She was disarmingly genuine, with a soft-spoken wisdom that made him feel both at home and exposed at the same time. She had a way of seeing right through him, of knowing exactly when to press and when to back off.

And yet, there was still something she wasn't telling him. He could feel it—like a secret she carried with her, hidden beneath the surface. Whenever the conversation veered too close to her past, Emily would close off, her eyes darkening, and the moment would slip away. Alex wasn't sure what it was, but he could sense that she was holding back, and it made him both curious and cautious.

It was a late afternoon when the moment finally came.

Alex had spent the day wandering through the town, trying to sort through the feelings that had become a constant presence in his life since meeting Emily. He had come to accept that there was something about her that was unlike anyone he had ever known—something raw and unfiltered. She was real, and that terrified him. The realness of it all was too much. He had spent his entire life hiding behind masks, behind facades that had shielded him from the vulnerability that Emily seemed to wear so naturally.

As he walked into the small café that had become his second home, he saw her sitting in the corner booth, her hair loose around her shoulders, a book resting on the table in front of her. She looked peaceful, content in a way that made his chest tighten. He had seen this side of her before, but today it felt different—something in the air, an unspoken tension that hummed between them, something that neither of them had acknowledged yet.

He approached the booth slowly, unsure of how to break the silence that always seemed to hang in the air between them.

She looked up as he approached, her eyes meeting his, and for a moment, the world seemed to stop. There was something in her gaze that made his heart skip—a familiarity, a warmth, but also a challenge. He didn't know what that challenge was, but he could feel it deep in his bones.

"Hey," he said, his voice softer than usual.

"Hey yourself," she replied, her smile small but genuine. "How's your day been?"

"Busy," Alex said, sliding into the booth across from her. He was lying, of course. His day had been anything but busy. But he didn't want to tell her about the swirl of thoughts that had kept him occupied, the growing sense of confusion he was trying to outrun. "You?"

"Same," she said, closing her book and setting it aside. Her eyes never left his, and Alex could see that she was studying him in that way she always did, as though trying to read the thoughts swirling in his mind. "You're looking a little... distracted today. More so than usual."

Alex paused, unsure of how to respond. She had a way of cutting to the heart of things without even trying. He could tell she was waiting for him to open up, but the walls he had built around himself were too thick for him to break down, even for her.

"I'm fine," he said quickly, forcing a smile. "Just... thinking."

Emily's gaze softened. She knew him too well. "Thinking about what?"

Alex swallowed. He wanted to tell her. He wanted to pour out all the confusion, all the self-doubt that had been bubbling inside of him since he arrived in town. But something stopped him. The truth about who he really was, the life he had left behind—he couldn't share that with her. Not yet. Not when he wasn't even sure who he was anymore.

"I'm not sure," he said, the words tasting foreign in his mouth. "Just… stuff."

"Stuff?" she repeated, arching an eyebrow. "Is that all?"

There it was again—the challenge. Emily wasn't going to let him off the hook so easily. She wasn't like the others. She wasn't content to let him hide behind his half-truths. And as much as he wanted to deflect, to retreat into the carefully constructed shell he had spent years perfecting, something in her made him want to try, to let her in.

"Okay," he said, leaning forward. "Maybe it's more than just stuff. Maybe I'm not sure who I'm supposed to be anymore."

Emily didn't say anything at first. She just looked at him, her expression unreadable. Then, after what seemed like an eternity, she spoke, her voice quiet and gentle.

"Who are you trying to be, Alex?" she asked. "The person you were before, or the person you want to be now?"

Her question struck him like a lightning bolt, and for a moment, Alex couldn't breathe. It was as though the air had been sucked out of the room. His mind raced, trying to process the depth of her words. The person he was before? Or the person he wanted to be now?

"I don't know," he admitted, his voice barely above a whisper. "I don't even know what that means anymore."

Emily reached across the table, placing her hand gently over his. The simple gesture sent a jolt through him, something electric and undeniable. There was no pretense in the way she touched him. No judgment. Just a quiet understanding.

"Maybe you don't have to have it all figured out," she said softly. "Maybe… maybe it's enough just to be who you are right now."

Alex felt the weight of her words settle over him. For the first time in weeks, he let himself feel something other than the anxiety that had been his constant companion. He didn't have to have it all figured out. He didn't have to be the man he thought he should be. He could just be… himself.

But the thought was fleeting. He wasn't sure who that person was anymore.

As he sat there, his mind reeling, he noticed that Emily's hand hadn't moved from his. It was as if she, too, was waiting for something to happen. She wasn't in a hurry. There was no rush to unravel the truth, no sense of urgency. Just the two of them, sitting in the quiet café, connected by something unspoken but powerful.

"I'm not good at this," he said after a long silence, pulling his hand away reluctantly.

Emily didn't seem offended. If anything, her expression softened even more. "Not good at what?"

"At being honest," Alex said, his voice rough with the confession. "I've spent my whole life lying. Hiding. Pretending to be someone I'm not."

Emily nodded slowly, as if she understood more than he was willing to admit. "I think we're all a little guilty of that, aren't we? Hiding parts of ourselves. But the question is—do we want to keep hiding?"

Alex sat back in his chair, a heavy sigh escaping his lips. "I don't know. I think… I think I want to stop hiding. But I'm scared."

"Scared of what?"

"Of losing everything," he said, his eyes meeting hers. "Of losing… you."

Emily blinked, as though his words had struck her deeper than he had intended. For a long moment, neither of them spoke. The weight of the silence seemed to press down on them, making everything feel more significant, more urgent.

Then, just as suddenly, Emily reached across the table again, this time taking his hand more firmly, her fingers wrapping around his. "You won't lose me, Alex," she said, her voice steady and sincere. "Not if you're honest. Not if you're brave enough to be yourself."

Alex stared at her, unable to find the words. Her hand in his felt like an anchor in the storm of his thoughts, a tether that kept him grounded, kept him tethered to something real, something true.

For the first time since he had arrived in this town, Alex didn't feel alone. And that scared him more than anything.

But as he sat there, looking into Emily's eyes, he realized something. Maybe, just maybe, he wasn't the only one hiding. Maybe there was more to her story, more that she was holding back, more that she wasn't telling him. And as much as he wanted to peel back the layers of his own past, he knew the time had come for him to start peeling back hers as well.

And so, as the last light of day faded from the sky, Alex Garrett—this new man who had come to this town to find himself—was faced with a choice. To keep running from the truth or to embrace the bond that had formed between him and Emily.

The choice was his.

Five

A Moment of Weakness

The autumn breeze rustled through the trees as Alex Garrett walked along the quiet streets of the town, his mind heavy with thoughts he couldn't shake. Each step seemed to echo louder than the last, a constant reminder of the unease he had been carrying for days now. His entire world had shifted since meeting Emily Clarke, and with every passing day, the foundations of the life he had built—the life he had created for himself—seemed to crumble a little more.

It had started with the simple truth of wanting to be seen for who he was, and not for the wealth that had defined him for so long. Emily had challenged him in ways he hadn't expected. She had made him question everything—the very essence of who he was. And in turn, he had started to ask himself what it would mean to let someone in. To let her in.

A Moment of Weakness

But what terrified him most wasn't the idea of loving her. It was the fear that he wasn't good enough for her—that, despite his best efforts, he would never be the man she deserved.

The more he tried to settle into this new life, the more the past clung to him, like a shadow he couldn't outrun. It wasn't just the memories that haunted him. It was the overwhelming pressure of maintaining the lie—the facade of being just an ordinary man. The truth lingered at the edge of his consciousness, threatening to tear everything apart. Emily didn't know who he really was. She didn't know the real Alex, the man who had once been a billionaire with an empire at his feet. But the guilt gnawed at him, and the longer he kept his secret, the more it felt like he was betraying her.

It was late evening when he found himself at the café again, sitting in the corner booth where he and Emily had spent so many quiet moments. The place was unusually empty tonight, the familiar hum of conversation absent. He liked it this way—peaceful, undisturbed—but tonight, the silence was suffocating. He hadn't seen Emily for two days, and despite his attempts to stay distracted, he couldn't help but wonder where she was, what she was doing. The last time they spoke, they had fallen into an uncomfortable silence, a crack in their easy banter that neither of them had addressed.

It was then that he saw her.

She entered through the door, her presence like a sudden rush of fresh air. Her hair was tied back into a loose ponytail, her face bare of makeup, and she looked effortlessly beautiful in a simple sweater and jeans. But there was something in the way she held herself, something that made her seem distant, as if a part of her had withdrawn. Alex felt a pang in his chest. He couldn't place it, but he knew that something was wrong. Something had changed.

She didn't see him at first, her gaze fixed on the counter as she ordered her coffee. But Alex couldn't look away. His heart raced in his chest as he watched her, trying to make sense of the whirlwind of emotions that had built up inside him. There was a part of him that wanted to run—to leave before she could get too close, before the truth could tear them apart. But another part of him, the part that had been longing for something real, something true, couldn't turn away.

As she turned to find a seat, her eyes landed on him. For a brief moment, their gazes locked, and the air between them seemed to crackle with unspoken tension. She hesitated, then made her way toward his table, her footsteps light but deliberate. Alex's breath caught in his throat as she sat across from him, her expression unreadable.

"Hey," she said quietly, her voice softer than usual. There was a hint of something in her tone—something that made Alex's pulse quicken. "How are you?"

"I'm fine," he said, forcing a smile. But it was hollow, a weak attempt at pretending everything was okay. The truth was, he wasn't fine. Far from it. The weight of his secret felt heavier than ever, pressing down on him with each passing day.

A Moment of Weakness

Emily studied him for a moment, her gaze lingering on his face as if trying to read the truth written there. She was good at that. Too good, sometimes.

"You don't look fine," she said softly. "What's going on, Alex?"

Alex felt a sharp pang in his chest at her words. He didn't want to open up, didn't want to let her in any deeper than he already had. But in that moment, he could feel the walls he had so carefully built starting to crack. It was as if her presence, her quiet understanding, was pulling him toward something he wasn't ready for. He had been holding his emotions at bay for so long, but now, in the quiet of the café, the floodgates were threatening to open.

"I... I don't know," he said, his voice barely above a whisper. "I've been thinking a lot lately. About everything. About who I am, and what I'm doing here." His hands tightened around the cup of coffee in front of him, as if trying to ground himself. "It's not easy pretending, Emily. Pretending that I'm someone I'm not."

Emily's eyes softened, and she reached across the table, placing her hand over his. The simple touch sent a jolt through him, a rush of warmth that he didn't expect. She didn't say anything for a long moment, just sat there, her fingers lightly brushing against his. The silence between them was thick with unspoken words, but in that moment, Alex felt more exposed than he ever had in his life.

"You don't have to pretend with me," she said quietly. Her voice was steady, but there was something vulnerable in the way she spoke. "You don't have to be someone else."

Alex swallowed hard. The weight of her words settled over him like a blanket, warm but suffocating. He wanted to believe her, wanted to believe that he could just be himself, without the constant fear of being discovered. But the truth was, he didn't know how. He didn't know who he was anymore. Not without his wealth, not without his status. He was just... Alex. A man who had once had everything and now had nothing. Or maybe he had something more than he'd ever realized—something that scared him even more than losing everything.

"Emily..." he began, his voice trembling slightly. He opened his mouth to say more, but the words got stuck. The fear that had been building inside him for weeks suddenly burst to the surface. The truth he had been hiding, the secret that had been eating away at him, felt like it was suffocating him.

Before he could stop himself, the words came spilling out.

"I'm not who you think I am," he blurted, his voice rough. "I'm not just Alex. I'm—" He stopped, his breath coming in shallow gasps. The confession was on the tip of his tongue, but he couldn't bring himself to say it. Not yet. Not like this.

Emily looked at him with wide, searching eyes, her hand still resting on his. She was waiting for him to continue, to explain. But Alex couldn't do it. The fear, the guilt, the shame—everything that had been building up inside him for so long—it all threatened to swallow him whole.

A Moment of Weakness

"I don't… I don't know what I'm doing," he said, his voice barely audible. "I don't know who I am anymore, and I don't know how to make it stop."

Emily didn't pull her hand away. Instead, she leaned in closer, her eyes softening as she spoke.

"Alex, whatever it is, you don't have to carry it alone," she said gently. "I'm here. I'm not going anywhere."

Her words were like a balm to his wounded soul, and for the first time in what felt like forever, Alex felt a flicker of hope. Maybe he wasn't as alone as he thought. Maybe, just maybe, there was a chance for him to be the man he had always wanted to be—someone worthy of her trust, someone worthy of her love.

But just as the thought began to take root, the walls inside him rose up again. He couldn't do it. Not yet. The fear was too strong, the weight of his past too heavy. He couldn't reveal the truth. Not when it felt like it would tear everything apart.

"I'm sorry," he said, pulling his hand away from hers, suddenly feeling exposed. "I don't know what's wrong with me."

Emily didn't argue, didn't push him. She just sat there, her gaze steady and unwavering, as though she were waiting for him to come to his own realization. She didn't speak. She didn't have to. The silence between them was more powerful than any words could have been.

Alex took a shaky breath, trying to pull himself together. His heart was racing, his hands trembling, but the moment of weakness had passed. For now, anyway. The truth was still lodged in his chest, like a heavy stone that he couldn't rid himself of. But Emily's quiet presence, her understanding without judgment, had given him something he hadn't expected.

A chance. A chance to confront his past. A chance to finally be the man he was meant to be.

And maybe, just maybe, a chance to let her see him for who he truly was.

Six

The Tipping Point

The quiet hum of the town had become familiar to Alex—comfortable, even. But the stillness of the streets now felt suffocating. He couldn't remember when his unease had first started to claw at him again, but he was acutely aware of it now. It was as if the ground beneath his feet had shifted once more, and he was no longer sure where he stood. There had been moments of clarity, moments when he thought he could escape the weight of his past and embrace this simple life, but they were fleeting. The truth was, he couldn't outrun who he was.

He had tried to avoid the inevitable. He had told himself that the past didn't matter—that it wasn't important who he had been. But every time Emily's gaze lingered on him a little too long, every time her voice softened with concern, the walls he had so carefully built to protect himself began to crumble.

Disguised in Poverty, Loved in Truth

He had to tell her the truth. But that truth was a dangerous thing—one that could destroy everything.

He hadn't seen Emily in two days. Her absence left a quiet ache inside him that was impossible to ignore. They had shared too many quiet moments, too many glimpses into each other's lives, to just let things slip back into the awkward distance that had defined so many of his past relationships. But every time he tried to reach out, the fear of losing her—of revealing who he truly was—kept him silent.

The tipping point came that afternoon when he saw her.

It was just after lunch when Alex spotted Emily from across the street. She was standing at the entrance to the bookstore, a bag of groceries at her side. She seemed lost in thought, her shoulders slightly hunched, as if carrying some invisible weight. Alex's heart clenched at the sight. She had always been so poised, so steady, but today there was something different in her demeanor—a heaviness he couldn't explain.

He hesitated for a moment, unsure if he should approach. But then, as if drawn by some unseen force, he found himself walking toward her. His feet seemed to move on their own, as if they knew something his mind couldn't comprehend. He needed to speak with her. Needed to know what had changed.

"Emily?" His voice came out quieter than he intended, but she heard him, turning toward him with a start.

Her eyes flickered, a brief flash of recognition, and then she

The Tipping Point

smiled—a tight, strained smile that didn't reach her eyes. "Alex," she said softly, her voice betraying none of the emotions Alex knew she was feeling. "I didn't expect to see you here."

"I've been around," he said, his voice sounding far too casual for the knot that had formed in his stomach. "Is everything alright?"

For a moment, she didn't answer. Instead, she shifted uncomfortably, glancing away. Alex's gaze softened as he noticed the subtle tremor in her hands, the way her fingers gripped the bag just a little too tightly. Something was wrong. He could sense it. But she wasn't saying anything, wasn't opening up the way she usually did.

"I'm fine," she finally said, her smile flickering again. "Just... busy, you know."

Alex didn't believe her. He could see the cracks in the façade she was trying to maintain. But he didn't press her—not immediately. There would be time for that later. What mattered now was that she was here, standing in front of him, and whatever distance had come between them in the past few days was about to be closed.

"Emily, you don't have to hide anything from me," he said quietly, his voice thick with unspoken emotion. "I don't care about the past, or what's happened before. I care about you."

Her eyes darted toward him, a flicker of something—anger, confusion, maybe even fear—passing over her face before it was quickly masked by a veneer of composure.

"Alex, please," she said, her tone sharp, her words cutting through the air like a blade. "You don't know anything about me. You don't know what I've been through."

The words hit him harder than he expected. It was a blow, a harsh reminder that, despite the connection they had shared, there was so much he didn't know about her—so much she wasn't willing to share. And yet, he couldn't shake the feeling that, in some way, they were both hiding from each other. That the truth was something neither of them was ready to face.

"I don't need to know everything," he said, his voice softer now, almost pleading. "I just want to be there for you. I want to know the real you."

The tension between them grew palpable. Emily's shoulders stiffened, and for a moment, Alex thought she might walk away. But instead, she took a deep breath, her gaze softening just a little. She didn't look at him, not directly, but instead stared down at the ground, her hands nervously fidgeting with the hem of her sweater.

"Alex, I…" Her voice faltered, and for a moment, he thought she might say something—something important, something that would finally allow them to break through the walls that had grown up between them. But then, just as quickly, her words disappeared. She straightened up and forced a smile. "I think I need some time, okay?"

The Tipping Point

Alex's heart dropped. He hadn't expected this—hadn't anticipated her pulling away so completely. There was something in her tone that told him this wasn't just a temporary distance. It was something deeper. Something that had shifted, something irrevocable.

"Emily, don't—" he began, but she cut him off before he could finish.

"I'm not the person you think I am," she said, her voice hard now, guarded. "I'm not the perfect picture you've created in your mind. And I'm not ready to let you in. Not yet."

Her words hung in the air between them like a heavy fog, suffocating him. He had always known that there was something she wasn't telling him. But now, in this moment, it felt like the truth was slipping further and further out of his reach. And the realization that she might never let him in—that she might never fully trust him—cut deeper than he could have imagined.

Alex opened his mouth to say something—anything—but the words died in his throat. He couldn't bring himself to argue with her, couldn't find the right words to convince her to stay, to trust him. She was already walking away, her back turned to him as she made her way down the street.

He stood there, frozen in place, watching her disappear into the distance. The moment that had been building between them, the fragile connection they had shared, had just shattered. And with it, something inside him had cracked wide open. A deep sense of loss settled over him, filling the empty space between his ribs like a weight he couldn't shake.

He had failed her. He had failed them both.

But there was something else, too. Something that gnawed at him, that told him this wasn't the end—not yet. Because, deep down, Alex knew that the real tipping point hadn't come yet. The secrets they both held, the things they weren't saying, had only just begun to surface.

The truth was, their worlds were about to collide in a way neither of them could prepare for. And when that truth came to light, there would be no turning back.

Seven

The Shadows of the Past

The soft glow of the streetlamp flickered as Alex Garrett walked through the quiet town, his thoughts as restless as the cool autumn wind that blew around him. His feet seemed to move on their own, following the familiar path he had walked countless times since arriving in this sleepy place. The town, which had once felt like an escape, now felt like a trap—a prison of his own making. The simple life he had hoped for, the peace he had sought, seemed to be slipping further out of his reach with every passing day.

But it wasn't just the weight of his own lies that had him feeling like he was drowning. It was Emily. She had pushed him away, her words lingering in his mind, haunting him. "I'm not the person you think I am." Her voice echoed in his ears, the finality in her tone clear. She had drawn a line, one he had crossed, and now it seemed impossible to step back across it.

Alex had always prided himself on being in control. He had built an empire, had surrounded himself with people who feared him, respected him, and who never questioned his authority. But now, here in this town, with Emily slipping further away, he felt the ground beneath him shift, as though the very foundations of his life had started to crumble. He was no longer the man he had been, but he was also not yet the man he wanted to become. He was caught between two versions of himself, and neither seemed to fit.

His phone buzzed in his pocket, snapping him from his thoughts. He pulled it out, seeing a message from Olivia, his former assistant, the one connection to the life he had left behind. She had been persistent in her attempts to reach him, but until now, he had been able to avoid the pull of his past. He read the message and felt the knot tighten in his stomach.

"Alex, I need to talk to you. It's urgent. Please call me when you can."

He stared at the screen, his finger hovering over the call button, but he couldn't bring himself to press it. He wasn't ready. The past, his old life, the empire he had once ruled, all of it seemed to lurk just beyond the horizon, waiting to swallow him whole. He couldn't face it—not yet. But he knew that it was coming, that the past would find a way to reach him eventually. And when it did, there would be no turning back.

As he stood there in the quiet street, his thoughts swirling, he saw a figure approaching in the distance. The silhouette was familiar, and a wave of dread washed over him as he recognized her. Emily.

She walked toward him, her pace slow, almost deliberate. There was a tension in the air between them, a distance that neither of them had been able to close. Alex's heart skipped a beat as she came closer, her features growing clearer in the dim light. She looked different somehow—distant, colder. The warmth that had once radiated from her seemed to have faded, replaced by something darker, more guarded.

"Emily," Alex said softly, his voice carrying an edge of uncertainty. He hadn't expected to see her tonight, hadn't expected to confront the fragile distance that had grown between them. But now that she was here, he didn't know how to bridge the gap.

She stopped a few feet away from him, her gaze locking with his. There was a flicker of something—uncertainty, maybe fear—but it was gone before Alex could fully read it. She seemed distant, as if she had built a wall between them that he couldn't tear down.

"You're still here," Emily said quietly, her voice devoid of warmth. "I thought you would have left by now."

The words stung more than he cared to admit, but he couldn't let her see how much they affected him. He had spent days trying to convince himself that he was better off without her, that he had nothing left to lose. But now, standing in front of her, he realized just how wrong he had been.

"I'm not going anywhere," Alex replied, his tone firmer than he felt. "But you've been avoiding me. Why?"

Emily took a deep breath, her eyes narrowing slightly. "I've been trying to protect myself," she said, her words heavy with meaning. "And you… you've been hiding from me. Hiding from the truth."

Alex's chest tightened at her words. She was right. He had been hiding from her, from everything she represented. The truth was, he had never truly trusted her. He had built up walls around himself so high that he couldn't see the ground beneath him. And now, Emily was confronting him with the very thing he had feared the most: the truth.

"I didn't mean to hurt you," Alex said, his voice raw with emotion. "I didn't mean for it to be this way. I never thought I'd—" He stopped himself, realizing that the words he wanted to say were not the ones that mattered. The truth, his truth, was something he had been avoiding for far too long. "There's something I need to tell you."

Emily didn't say anything, just watched him with guarded eyes, waiting for him to continue. Her silence urged him on, but the fear gripped him like a vise, squeezing the air out of his lungs.

"I'm not who you think I am," Alex finally said, the words tumbling out before he could stop them. "I've lied to you. About everything."

The air between them seemed to crackle with tension as Emily took a step back, her eyes widening in disbelief. "What do you mean? What are you talking about, Alex?"

The floodgates had opened, and there was no turning back now. He had to tell her the truth. The entire truth.

"I'm not just Alex Garrett," he said, his voice trembling. "I'm Alexander Greyson. The heir to Greyson Technologies. I built the company from the ground up, and I've been hiding behind this new identity because I wanted to be… someone else. Someone who wasn't defined by the money and the power I've had my entire life."

Emily's face went pale, and Alex watched as the realization hit her like a tidal wave. She took another step back, her hands trembling as she tried to process what he had just said.

"Why didn't you tell me?" she whispered, her voice hoarse. "Why didn't you trust me enough to tell me the truth?"

Alex didn't have an answer. He couldn't explain why he had kept this secret for so long, why he had allowed the lies to build up between them. He had told himself that it was for her own good, that if he revealed who he really was, she would leave him. But now, standing before her, the truth felt heavier than ever. And in that moment, he realized that his fear had been a cage, one that had trapped him in a life he no longer wanted.

"I was afraid," Alex admitted, his voice barely above a whisper. "Afraid that if you knew the truth, you would walk away. Afraid that I would lose you."

Emily looked at him, her expression unreadable. There was a long silence between them, the weight of his confession hanging in the air like a suffocating cloud. For a moment, Alex thought she might walk away, might never speak to him again. But then, she took a deep breath, her shoulders relaxing ever so slightly.

"I need time," she said quietly. "I don't know if I can... if I can forgive you for this, Alex. I don't know if I can trust you again."

The words hit him harder than he had expected. He had prepared himself for anger, for betrayal, but hearing her say it so calmly, so matter-of-factly, shattered him. He had spent so long pretending to be someone else, hiding behind the lies and the walls he had built, that he had never considered the cost. The truth had finally caught up with him, and now there was no escaping it.

"I understand," Alex said, his voice barely audible. "I didn't deserve your trust. But I'm not running anymore, Emily. I'm not hiding. If you can't forgive me, I'll understand. But I can't go back to the way things were."

She nodded, her eyes glistening with unshed tears. "I don't know if I can be what you want, Alex. I don't know if I can live with the fact that you've been hiding this from me all along."

Alex reached out, his hand trembling as he touched her arm. "I don't expect you to forgive me right away. I just needed you to know the truth. I couldn't keep lying to you, to myself."

She didn't pull away from him, but she didn't lean into him

either. The space between them was still too vast, the distance too wide. Emily stared at him for a long moment before speaking again.

"I need to think," she said softly. "I need to figure out what this all means."

And with that, she turned and walked away, leaving Alex standing in the cold, the weight of his confession settling over him like a heavy fog.

The past had caught up with him. The shadows that had once seemed so distant now loomed large, their presence overwhelming. And as Emily disappeared into the night, Alex knew that whatever happened next, their world would never be the same.

Eight

Breaking Point

The days following that fateful conversation with Emily felt like a blur to Alex. The silence between them was suffocating, a chasm that seemed to grow wider with each passing moment. He had hoped, foolishly, that revealing the truth—his truth—would set things right between them. But instead, it had fractured everything. The lies he had built his life around had crumbled in an instant, and now, he was left standing at the edge of an emotional abyss, unsure if he would ever be able to pull himself out.

He hadn't heard from Emily in two days. Not a single word. She hadn't returned his calls, hadn't answered his messages. It was as though she had disappeared from his life entirely, vanishing into the same quiet town that had once felt like a refuge. He told himself that he should be patient, that she needed time to process everything he had revealed, but patience had never been his strong suit. The anxiety gnawed at him, a constant presence in the back of his mind. Every time he saw her face, every time he remembered the way she had looked at him after his confession, he felt the weight of his mistake all over again.

But what terrified him more than anything was the possibility that she might never forgive him. That the trust they had built, so fragile and new, might be irreparably shattered.

It was late afternoon when Alex found himself at the café, the same café where he had spent so many quiet moments with Emily. The place was nearly empty, save for a couple sitting in the corner, their voices low, and the barista cleaning the counter behind the counter. The smell of freshly brewed coffee filled the air, but it did little to calm the storm inside him.

He had hoped to see her here. He had hoped that, after everything, she might return to the place where they had first connected. But as the minutes ticked by, and still no sign of Emily, a sinking feeling settled in his chest. The silence between them had stretched so long, so painfully thin, that it felt impossible to repair.

Alex's phone buzzed in his pocket, snapping him from his thoughts. He pulled it out, praying that it was Emily. But when he saw the message, his heart sank.

It was from Olivia.

"Alex, we need to talk. It's urgent. I'm on my way to meet you now."

Urgent. The word lingered in his mind, sending a chill down his spine. He had spent the last few days trying to distance himself from his past, from the life he had left behind, but now it seemed that the past was catching up with him faster than he had anticipated. He had been avoiding Olivia's calls for days, but he couldn't avoid her forever. Whatever it was that she wanted to tell him, he knew it couldn't be good.

The café's door opened with a soft chime, and Alex looked up to see Olivia walking in. She was dressed in a sleek black jacket, her blonde hair tied back in a tight ponytail. She looked every bit the professional—confident, poised, and completely unaffected by the weight of the tension in the room. But as soon as her eyes met his, the walls she had built up between them seemed to crumble.

"Alex," she said, her voice tight, her usual businesslike demeanor slipping just slightly. "We need to talk."

He stood up, his heart pounding in his chest. "What's going on? What's this about?"

Olivia glanced around the room before nodding to a nearby table. "Let's sit down first. I don't want to cause a scene."

They moved to the table, and Olivia slid into the seat across from him, her hands folded tightly in front of her. Alex could see the tension in her posture, the way her jaw was set, as if she were preparing for something difficult. His stomach churned, his mind racing as he tried to piece together what had happened.

"I've been trying to reach you," Olivia began, her voice clipped. "But you've been avoiding me, and I couldn't sit around waiting anymore. There's something I need to tell you—something important."

Alex swallowed hard, his mind already jumping to conclusions. "What is it? What's going on?"

Olivia hesitated, her eyes briefly flickering to the side. "It's about Greyson Technologies. We've hit a major roadblock. There's been a leak—someone inside the company has been leaking information to the competition. And it's worse than we thought, Alex. It's not just about the business; it's personal."

Alex's blood ran cold. The words hit him like a punch to the gut. He had been hoping, desperately hoping, that his old life would stay in the past. That he could escape the shadow of the empire he had built. But now, it seemed that everything was unraveling, faster than he could keep up with.

"Who is it?" he asked, his voice low and strained. "Who's doing this?"

Olivia's eyes darkened. "I don't know yet. But we're investigating. And the worst part is, the leaks are connected to you, Alex. There's talk that someone close to you—someone you trust—has been feeding information to our rivals."

The words hit him like a tidal wave. He had always known that his past wouldn't stay buried forever, but to hear it all laid out in front of him was another thing entirely. The weight of it pressed down on him, suffocating him with the realization that his secret life was starting to bleed into this one. And there was no escaping it.

Alex ran a hand through his hair, his mind racing. "What do you mean, 'someone close to me'? Who's been leaking information?"

Olivia's gaze flickered toward the door, and she lowered her voice. "We have reason to believe that it's someone within the company who has a personal connection to you. Someone who's been keeping tabs on you ever since you left. And now, they're using that connection to sabotage the business."

Alex's heart skipped a beat. The thought that someone—someone he had trusted—might be betraying him sent a wave of anger through him. But it was more than that. It was fear. Fear that the very thing he had tried to escape—his past—was coming back to haunt him, dragging him back into a world he had fought so hard to leave behind.

"Who?" Alex demanded, his voice rising. "Who is it?"

Olivia hesitated again, as if weighing her next words carefully. Finally, she spoke, her voice barely above a whisper. "It's Emily."

The name hit him like a punch to the stomach. Emily? No, that couldn't be right. It didn't make sense. She had no connection to his past—at least, that's what he had thought. But now, as the weight of her actions settled over him, the possibility seemed more and more real.

"No," Alex whispered, shaking his head. "That's impossible. Emily would never do that."

Olivia's face remained impassive. "I know it's hard to believe. But the evidence is stacking up. We've found links between her and the people who are behind the leaks. She's been involved, Alex. And right now, she's the one person who could bring everything crashing down."

Alex's mind spun, the ground beneath him seeming to tilt and spin. His thoughts were a jumbled mess of confusion and disbelief. Emily had been so honest with him. So real. There was no way she could be involved in something like this. He had seen the vulnerability in her eyes, the way she had opened up to him. He had trusted her. He had wanted her to be part of his life—no, his new life. And now, this.

He stood up abruptly, the chair scraping against the floor. "I have to go," he said, his voice strained. "I need to see her."

Olivia didn't try to stop him. She only watched as he walked toward the door, her eyes filled with something unreadable. She knew something he didn't—knew the truth about Emily's involvement in his past. But Alex wasn't ready to face that truth. Not yet.

As he stepped out into the cool evening air, his chest tightened with the weight of everything that had just been revealed. The betrayal, the lies, the secrets—all of it crashing down on him. And Emily… Emily, the one person he had allowed himself to care about, had been keeping secrets of her own.

He didn't know what he would find when he confronted her, but he knew one thing for sure: whatever happened next, his life would never be the same.

The breaking point had arrived. And nothing would ever be the same again.

Nine

Secrets Exposed

The town was shrouded in an eerie stillness as Alex Garrett walked down the familiar streets, his mind spinning in a whirlpool of confusion and rage. The weight of Olivia's revelation had crushed him—every word she spoke reverberating in his chest like a beating drum. Emily. The woman he had come to trust, the woman who had become so integral to his new life, had been hiding something. And that something was far more dangerous than he had imagined.

As the sun dipped below the horizon, casting the world into shadows, Alex's steps quickened. He had to see her. He had to confront her and get to the heart of this betrayal. His thoughts collided with each other, each one more painful than the last. How could Emily, the woman who had seemed so honest, so vulnerable, have been hiding this? Why would she involve herself in something so devastating, so treacherous?

He didn't know what he was going to say when he found her, or how he was going to face her after everything that had been exposed. But he couldn't let this fester. He needed answers, and he needed them now.

The small town's main street felt empty tonight, the usual hum of activity subdued by the gathering twilight. Alex's heart pounded in his chest as he approached the bookstore, the same place where he had first seen Emily—a place where they had shared their lives, their hopes, and their fears. But now, all of that seemed like a distant memory, tainted by the revelation that Emily had been a part of the scheme to destroy the very empire he had been trying to leave behind.

As he approached the door, his hand trembled, uncertainty and anger making his pulse race. He had told himself that he wouldn't go back to the world he had left behind, that he wouldn't let his past define him. But now, it seemed inevitable. The past was clawing its way back into his life, and Emily was at the center of it all. Could he trust her again? Could he ever truly believe her words, her promises, after this?

The bell above the door jingled as he stepped inside. The bookstore was quiet, the faint smell of paper and dust lingering in the air. Emily was behind the counter, her back to him as she rearranged some books on the shelf. When she heard the door, she turned, and her eyes widened in surprise when she saw him standing there. Her smile faltered for a brief moment, before she quickly masked it with a neutral expression.

"Alex," she said, her voice guarded. "What are you doing here?"

"I need to talk to you," he said, his voice firm, but with an edge of desperation. "Now."

Emily's face tightened, and for a brief moment, Alex saw a flicker of something—fear? Guilt?—cross her features. It was gone in an instant, replaced by the calm composure she usually wore so effortlessly. But Alex had seen enough. He could tell that something was off. She wasn't the woman he thought she was.

She set the books down and slowly walked toward him, her movements deliberate. "I don't think this is a good time," she said, her voice low. "Maybe we can talk tomorrow."

"No," Alex said, his voice rising. "We need to talk now. I know what's going on. I know about the leaks. I know about you."

Her face paled slightly, and for the first time since he had met her, Alex saw a crack in her facade. He could see the panic in her eyes, the hesitation that lingered just beneath the surface. Emily opened her mouth to say something, but no words came out. Instead, she took a step back, her hands shaking slightly.

"You don't understand," she said quietly, her voice trembling with emotion. "I didn't mean for it to happen this way. I never wanted any of this."

Alex's heart skipped a beat. Her words struck him like a slap in the face. "I didn't mean for it to happen this way." It sounded like a confession, a plea for understanding. But there was no understanding to be had. Not after everything that had been exposed. Not after the lies she had told him.

"No?" Alex asked, his voice dripping with bitterness. "Then what was all of this? What was the point of everything we shared? Were you just playing me from the beginning? Were you just trying to get close to me so you could use me?"

Emily recoiled slightly at the accusation, her eyes brimming with tears. "No, Alex," she whispered, her voice breaking. "It wasn't like that. I never meant to hurt you. I swear to you."

"Then what is it, Emily?" Alex demanded, his frustration boiling over. "How could you be involved in something like this? How could you betray me like this?"

There was a long, painful silence between them as Emily took a deep breath, clearly struggling to find the right words. Finally, she spoke, her voice barely a whisper. "I wasn't trying to hurt you. I was trying to protect you."

Alex's brow furrowed in confusion. "Protect me? From what? From the truth?"

Emily nodded slowly, her gaze never leaving his. "Yes. From the truth. You don't know the full story, Alex. There are things about me, things about my past, that you don't know. Things that I've been running from for a long time."

Alex felt a chill run down his spine. Her words hung in the air between them, thick with implication. What was she hiding? What was the truth that she had been so desperate to keep from him?

"What things?" Alex asked, his voice softening, but still laced with suspicion. "What truth are you talking about?"

Emily hesitated, her lips trembling as if the words were stuck in her throat. She took a step back, her shoulders slumping with the weight of whatever it was she was about to reveal. "I wasn't just some innocent bystander in all of this, Alex. I didn't just get caught up in something I didn't understand. I was involved. I knew about the leaks. I knew they were happening, and I was asked to help."

Alex's mind reeled at her words. "You knew?" he repeated, the disbelief rising in his chest. "You were a part of it? You were helping them sabotage my company?"

She nodded, her face filled with anguish. "I didn't want to. I swear to you. But I had no choice. I was threatened, Alex. I was being blackmailed."

"By who?" Alex asked, his voice low with fury. "Who would do that to you?"

Emily looked down at the floor, her eyes brimming with unshed tears. "By someone I once trusted. Someone close to me. They told me that if I didn't help them, they would expose my past—everything I had worked so hard to leave behind. I thought if I helped them, it would all go away. But now it's all coming back. And I never wanted you to be part of it. I never wanted you to get hurt."

Disguised in Poverty, Loved in Truth

The world seemed to tilt beneath Alex's feet as the full weight of her confession crashed over him. Emily had been a part of the conspiracy, yes, but she hadn't been a willing participant. She had been coerced, blackmailed into betraying him and his company. The realization stunned him—stunned him more than the betrayal itself.

"Who is it, Emily?" he asked, his voice barely above a whisper. "Who's been pulling your strings? Who's been using you to destroy everything I've worked for?"

Emily's face twisted in pain, her eyes dark with regret. "It's my brother," she said softly. "He's the one behind all of this. He's been working with the competitors. He used me to get to you, to get to Greyson Technologies."

The shock of her words hit Alex like a slap to the face. Emily had a brother—a person who had been pulling the strings from behind the scenes, using his sister as a pawn in a dangerous game. Alex's heart pounded in his chest as the pieces of the puzzle began to fall into place. This wasn't just about business rivalry; this was personal. And Emily had been caught in the crossfire.

"I'm so sorry, Alex," she whispered, her voice trembling. "I never wanted any of this to happen. I never wanted to hurt you. But now, everything is falling apart, and I don't know how to fix it."

Alex stood there, rooted to the spot, unable to move. His mind was a blur of conflicting emotions—anger, disbelief, and an aching sense of betrayal. But beneath it all, there was a glimmer

Secrets Exposed

of something else—something he hadn't expected. Compassion. For the first time, he saw the full picture. Emily hadn't been his enemy; she had been a victim, just like him. And yet, the damage had already been done. The trust between them had been shattered, and the consequences of her actions were impossible to ignore.

"I don't know what to say," Alex said, his voice heavy with emotion. "I don't know if I can forgive you for this, Emily. You've kept this from me. You've lied to me."

"I know," she whispered, her voice breaking. "I know I don't deserve your forgiveness. But please believe me when I say that I never wanted this. I never wanted to hurt you."

Alex took a deep breath, trying to steady himself. He had to make a choice—whether to walk away from everything he had believed in, or to try and salvage whatever was left between them.

The truth had been exposed, and there was no going back. But for the first time in a long while, Alex realized that maybe, just maybe, there was room for forgiveness.

Ten

The Cost of Truth

The night air felt cold against Alex's skin as he stood outside Emily's bookstore, his breath coming in shallow gasps. He had asked for the truth, demanded it, but now that it had been laid bare before him, he wasn't sure he could bear the weight of it. Emily's confession had shattered everything he thought he knew about her. She hadn't just been a bystander in the chaos that had threatened his empire—she had been a part of it. And the betrayal cut deeper than he could have imagined.

Her brother. The person she had trusted most in the world, the person she had once looked up to, had been the mastermind behind the leaks. It made sense, in a way, but it didn't make it any easier to accept. Emily had been trapped in a game of manipulation, forced to play a part she had never wanted. She had lied, yes, but there had been no malice in it. She had been cornered, her hands tied by the threat of losing everything she had worked for—and yet, the betrayal was undeniable.

Alex couldn't move, couldn't think straight. His mind was a tangle of anger, hurt, and confusion. He wanted to walk away, to leave this town and never look back, to wash his hands of the lies and deception. But as much as he wanted to run, he knew that he couldn't. The truth had been exposed, and now he had to face the consequences.

His phone buzzed in his pocket, pulling him from his spiraling thoughts. He pulled it out, his eyes narrowing when he saw Olivia's name on the screen. He had been avoiding her for days, but now, with the weight of Emily's confession pressing down on him, he couldn't avoid it any longer. With a deep breath, he answered the call.

"Alex," Olivia's voice was tight with urgency. "I need you to come to the office. We've got a problem."

"What is it?" Alex's voice was hoarse, the fatigue of the day taking its toll on him.

"It's about the leaks," Olivia continued, her words clipped. "We've tracked them to a source inside the company. Someone high up. We've got a name."

Alex's heart skipped a beat, but he didn't know whether it was from relief or dread. Emily had told him it was her brother, but hearing the confirmation from Olivia made everything feel too real.

"Who is it?" Alex asked, his voice barely above a whisper.

"It's Charlie Greyson," Olivia said. "Your uncle."

The words hit him like a physical blow. Charlie Greyson. The man who had helped raise him, the man who had always been there when Alex needed advice, guidance, and mentorship. His own flesh and blood. His uncle had been the one leaking the information, feeding the competitors, undermining everything Alex had worked for. The revelation felt like a betrayal of the deepest kind—a family member, someone he had trusted completely, had stabbed him in the back.

Alex's mind reeled. How had he missed it? How had he not seen the signs? Charlie had always been the quiet one, the one who had stayed in the background, content to let Alex take the spotlight. But now, it seemed that the man he had admired and looked up to had been working against him the entire time.

"Are you sure?" Alex asked, his voice a mixture of disbelief and rage.

"We've got the proof, Alex," Olivia replied, her voice grim. "We've traced the leaks back to his office. We're moving in on him as we speak."

Alex stood there, his legs feeling like jelly beneath him. He wanted to shout, to scream, to tear everything down, but he couldn't. He was frozen, paralyzed by the truth that had been laid bare before him. The people he had trusted, the people who had been closest to him, had been using him all along. His uncle. Emily's brother. It felt like the world was spinning out of control, and Alex was powerless to stop it.

"I'll be there in a few minutes," Alex said, his voice flat, devoid of emotion. He hung up without another word and stood there for a moment, staring at the empty street in front of him. The cost of truth had been revealed, and it was far more than he had ever imagined.

He knew he had to go to the office, that there was no avoiding it. But before he left, there was one more thing he had to do. He had to see Emily. He needed to hear it from her—needed to understand why she had kept the truth from him, why she had chosen to stay silent for so long. He needed closure, if only for his own peace of mind.

As he walked back toward the bookstore, his mind raced with questions. Could he forgive her? Could he forgive her brother? He had spent the last few days convincing himself that Emily was the one person he could trust, the one person who had shown him what it meant to be real. But now, as everything unraveled, it seemed like he had been living in a fantasy world, a dream that had been shattered by the harsh light of reality.

When he reached the bookstore, the door was still unlocked, and the bell above it jingled as he stepped inside. Emily was sitting behind the counter, her back to him. She didn't look up as he entered, as if she knew he was coming but didn't know what to say. Alex took a deep breath before walking up to her.

"Emily," he said softly, his voice barely above a whisper.

She turned slowly, her face pale, her eyes red from what Alex assumed were tears. She looked exhausted, as if the weight of everything had taken its toll on her. When her eyes met his, there was a flicker of guilt, of regret. But there was also something else—something deeper, something that Alex couldn't quite understand.

"Alex," she said, her voice small, almost timid. "I didn't think you'd come back."

"I needed to hear it from you," Alex replied, his voice rough. "I needed to know the truth."

Emily closed her eyes for a moment, as if steeling herself for the storm that was coming. "I told you everything, Alex. I told you what I could."

"No," he said, shaking his head. "You didn't tell me everything. You didn't tell me about your brother. About what he did."

Emily's eyes widened, and for a moment, Alex saw fear flash across her face. "How did you—"

"Olivia called," Alex interrupted, his voice cold. "She told me everything. About the leaks, about Charlie. About what you've been hiding."

Emily looked away, her hands trembling as she clasped them in her lap. "I never wanted you to find out this way," she said quietly. "I never wanted to drag you into this. I was trying to protect you. I was trying to protect myself."

The Cost of Truth

Alex felt his anger rise, but he forced it down, forcing himself to remain calm. "You protected yourself by lying to me. By keeping things from me. And now, because of you—because of your brother—I'm losing everything."

Emily stood up abruptly, her hands reaching out to him. "Alex, please. I never wanted this to happen. I never wanted you to get hurt."

Alex took a step back, his eyes hardening. "But I am hurt, Emily. You don't get to keep me in the dark, to make decisions for me without my consent. You should have told me the truth, from the beginning. If you had, maybe we wouldn't be here right now."

There was a long silence between them, the air thick with unspoken words. Emily's shoulders slumped, and for the first time, Alex saw her completely exposed. The woman he had trusted, the woman he had come to care for, was now the one person who had torn his world apart. He had believed in her, believed that she was different, that she could be his anchor in a world filled with uncertainty. But now, that belief seemed like a distant memory.

"I'm sorry," Emily whispered, her voice barely audible. "I never meant to hurt you. I never meant for any of this to happen."

Alex closed his eyes for a moment, trying to steady himself. He had wanted to hear her say those words, to hear her apologize, but now that they were out in the open, they didn't bring him any peace. The cost of truth was greater than he had ever imagined. The lies, the deceit, the betrayal—it was all too much. And he wasn't sure if he could ever forgive her for it.

"I need to go," Alex said finally, his voice thick with emotion. "I need to figure out what comes next."

And with that, he turned and walked out of the bookstore, the door swinging closed behind him. The truth had been exposed, but the price of it had left him broken, shattered, and lost in a world that no longer felt like his own.

The cost of truth had been more than he could bear. And now, as the weight of the world settled on his shoulders, Alex knew that nothing would ever be the same again.

Eleven

The Struggle for Redemption

The cold morning air hit Alex's face as he stepped out of the cab, his breath visible in the frigid wind. The towering glass building of Greyson Technologies loomed ahead, its modern façade a stark contrast to the storm brewing inside him. He hadn't wanted to come here, but he knew that he had no choice. The decision to return to the very place that had once been his life's foundation had been forced upon him by circumstances beyond his control. And as much as he wanted to walk away, to disappear into the anonymity of a life without Greyson Technologies, he couldn't. Not yet.

His hands were clenched into fists at his sides, the tension in his chest threatening to crush him with every step he took toward the entrance. Every inch of the glass doors reflected the man he had become: a man whose life had been shattered, whose trust had been betrayed, and whose heart had been broken.

But that wasn't the worst of it. The worst part was the man he was becoming—the man who had once prided himself on being in control, on being above reproach, but who now found himself struggling to hold onto the fragments of a life he didn't recognize.

His phone buzzed in his pocket, snapping him from his thoughts. He pulled it out and saw a message from Olivia.

"We've got the latest intel on your uncle. He's not going to go down without a fight. Be careful."

Alex read the message twice, the weight of her words sinking in deeper with each passing second. Charlie Greyson. His uncle. The man who had been like a father to him, who had helped him build the empire Alex had thought was indestructible. The man who had betrayed him, and who was now doing everything in his power to destroy the company Alex had worked so hard to save.

A bitter laugh escaped him as he shoved his phone back into his pocket. He had thought he understood the game of power and influence, but now he was forced to reckon with a deeper, more painful truth—nothing in his life had ever been what it seemed. And the people he had trusted most had only been using him, manipulating him for their own gain.

He approached the elevator bank, pressing the button with a sense of finality. The hum of the elevator was deafening, the sound of his own heartbeat thumping in his ears. He didn't know what he was walking into. He didn't know how the

The Struggle for Redemption

confrontation with Charlie would go, or whether he could even trust Olivia anymore. But one thing was certain—he couldn't keep running. Not anymore.

The elevator doors opened with a soft ding, and he stepped inside. His reflection in the polished steel doors seemed almost foreign to him. He didn't recognize the man staring back at him—the man who had once been so sure of his purpose, so confident in his place in the world. Now, all that was left was a man caught between two worlds: the one he had left behind and the one he was trying to rebuild. But the past didn't let go so easily. It clung to him like a shadow, refusing to release its grip.

When the elevator doors opened on the top floor, Alex stepped out into the familiar, sterile environment of Greyson Technologies. The sleek, modern interior greeted him with the same cold indifference it always had. But today, everything felt different. Every step he took echoed in the silence, reminding him of how far he had fallen from the man he had once been.

He passed his old office, the door slightly ajar, and for a moment, he considered going in. But the thought of walking into the space where he had once held all the power, where his decisions had shaped the future of the company, felt like a betrayal of everything he had fought to leave behind. Instead, he turned toward the glass-walled conference room at the end of the hall. Inside, he could see Olivia, her face a mask of concentration as she spoke to a few of the remaining executives.

He entered the room, and the conversation halted as all eyes turned toward him. Olivia's gaze lingered on him for a brief moment before she nodded to the others, signaling them to leave.

"I thought you'd be here soon," she said quietly, her tone more subdued than usual.

Alex didn't respond immediately. He glanced at the large conference table, his eyes briefly lingering on the empty chair at the head. He had once sat in that chair, calling the shots, making the decisions that had impacted the lives of so many. But now, it felt like a seat for someone else, a seat for a man who didn't belong.

"What's the situation?" Alex asked, his voice tight.

Olivia took a deep breath, her gaze flickering to the door before she spoke. "We've got enough evidence to take Charlie down. But he's got resources—people who are loyal to him. He's not going to make it easy. He's already moving behind the scenes, trying to cover his tracks."

Alex's heart sank as the reality of the situation hit him. His uncle was a seasoned businessman, a man who had built an empire just as powerful as the one Alex had inherited. He wasn't going to go down without a fight. And the stakes had never been higher.

"I need to see him," Alex said, his voice harder than he intended. "I need to hear it from him. I need to know why."

The Struggle for Redemption

Olivia didn't look surprised. She had known Alex would want to confront his uncle. She knew how much Charlie's betrayal had cut him.

"Are you sure about this?" Olivia asked, her voice laced with concern. "This could end badly, Alex. Charlie is dangerous, and he's not going to hold back."

Alex turned toward her, his eyes steely with determination. "I don't have a choice. I have to know what happened. I have to know why my own flesh and blood would do this."

There was a long pause before Olivia nodded, the resignation in her eyes clear. "I'll arrange the meeting," she said. "But be careful. He won't be as easy to control as you think."

The next hour passed in a blur as Olivia made the necessary arrangements. Charlie's office was located on the top floor of the building, a place Alex had visited countless times when he had first taken over the company. But now, the familiar surroundings felt cold and distant. As Alex made his way to the elevator, he could feel the weight of everything pressing down on him—the betrayal, the lies, the shattered trust—and he wasn't sure if he could bear it.

When the elevator doors opened, Alex stepped out into the luxurious hallway that led to Charlie's office. The door was slightly cracked, and through the gap, Alex could see his uncle sitting behind his desk, his hands folded neatly in front of him. Charlie's once-thriving empire now seemed like a gilded cage—a cage that Alex had been trapped in for far too long.

Alex pushed the door open and stepped inside. Charlie didn't look up immediately, but when he did, the look on his face was one of quiet recognition, tinged with something else—something darker.

"Alex," Charlie said, his voice smooth and calculating. "I was wondering when you'd show up."

Alex's fists clenched at his sides. "I want answers, Charlie. I want to know why you did it. Why you betrayed me. Why you tried to destroy everything I've worked for."

Charlie leaned back in his chair, his fingers steepled together. "Betrayal, Alex? You think I betrayed you? You were never ready to lead this company. I was just making sure it stayed in the right hands."

Alex's stomach churned at his uncle's words. "The 'right hands'? You mean your hands. You were never interested in me running this company. You've been trying to take it back from the start."

Charlie's lips curled into a cold smile. "You were too green, too naive. You thought you could just come in and take over like some savior. But the reality is, Alex, you're not built for this. You never were."

Alex's heart pounded in his chest, rage and betrayal flooding him in equal measure. He had always looked up to Charlie, had trusted him with everything. But now, as the truth unfolded before him, he saw his uncle for what he truly was: a man who would stop at nothing to maintain control, even if it meant destroying the people who trusted him.

"I trusted you," Alex said, his voice raw with emotion. "I looked up to you, Charlie. You were the one person who was supposed to be on my side."

Charlie's expression softened, but it wasn't sympathy Alex saw. It was pity. "You were never meant to take over, Alex. You're too young, too idealistic. I was doing you a favor, whether you realize it or not."

Alex's fists trembled with the weight of his fury, but he refused to let Charlie see him break. "This ends now. You're done."

Charlie's eyes gleamed with something dangerous, a glimmer of the man he had once been—the man who was willing to destroy everything for the sake of power. "It doesn't end here, Alex. This is just the beginning. You'll learn soon enough that power doesn't come easy. It's a game, and you were never cut out for it."

As Alex turned to leave, he realized the cost of truth had already been paid. Charlie had shown him the man he truly was, a man who had been willing to burn everything to the ground for the sake of his own ambition. But the truth, as painful as it was, had given Alex something else—something that had been missing for far too long: clarity.

This was the moment where everything changed. The struggle for redemption wasn't over, but it had begun. And Alex knew that no matter what happened next, he would never be the same again.

Twelve

A Test of Faith

The sun had barely risen, casting a dim light over the city as Alex stood at the window of his office, staring out at the horizon. The city seemed quieter than usual, its pulse slow and steady, but Alex's mind was a storm, chaotic and relentless. The night before had been a whirlwind of emotions—rage, disbelief, and something deeper that he couldn't name. He had confronted Charlie, the man who had betrayed him, the man who had tried to undermine everything Alex had worked for. But now, as the day stretched before him, he wasn't sure what to do next.

Charlie had been right about one thing: power was a game. But it wasn't a game Alex wanted to play anymore. He had spent so many years running in circles, trying to prove himself to a world that had never truly cared about him. And now, as the pieces of his life began to fall into place, Alex realized that the game he had been playing had never been about winning. It had been about survival. And in that game, there were no true winners. Only the ones who were willing to lose everything to get what they wanted.

He turned from the window, his gaze falling on the desk that had once been the center of his world. Papers, contracts, and reminders of the empire he had built lay scattered across it, but they no longer held the same power over him. The phone on the desk buzzed, breaking the silence, and Alex picked it up. The caller ID read Olivia's name.

He hesitated for a moment before answering. He didn't know what to expect from her, didn't know if she would still trust him after everything that had happened. But he had no choice. He had to face her, just as he had to face the mess that his life had become.

"Alex," Olivia's voice came through the phone, crisp and professional, but there was an underlying tension in her tone. "We need to talk."

"I know," Alex replied, his voice rough. "I need to see you. Can you come to the office?"

"I'm already on my way," she said. "I'll be there in ten minutes."

Alex hung up the phone and sat down at his desk, his hands trembling slightly. He had known Olivia for years—trusted her, relied on her—but after everything that had happened, he wasn't sure where they stood anymore. She had always been the one to guide him, to keep him grounded when he felt like he was losing control. But now, after the confrontation with Charlie and the devastating truth that had come to light, Alex wasn't sure if there was anything left to salvage. He had betrayed her trust, just as he had betrayed Emily's. The weight of it all seemed unbearable.

Ten minutes later, Olivia walked into his office, her presence filling the room with an undeniable authority. She was dressed in a sharp business suit, her expression as unreadable as ever. But Alex could see the weariness in her eyes, the quiet pain that lingered just beneath the surface.

"You wanted to see me?" Olivia said, her voice steady but tinged with a hint of concern.

Alex took a deep breath, trying to steady himself. "I don't know where to start," he admitted, his voice barely above a whisper. "Everything's falling apart, Olivia. I don't know how to fix it."

Olivia crossed the room and sat down across from him, folding her hands on the desk. Her eyes softened slightly, but she didn't speak immediately. She let the silence hang between them, allowing Alex to gather his thoughts.

"I've spent so much time building this empire," Alex continued, his voice thick with emotion. "I thought I was doing the right thing. I thought I was in control. But now, I'm not even sure what any of this means anymore."

"You're not alone in this," Olivia said, her voice low but steady.

"You've never been alone, Alex. We've all been here, working with you, building this company together. It's not just your responsibility."

Alex shook his head, his frustration bubbling to the surface. "It's always been my responsibility, Olivia. I've been the one making the decisions. I've been the one carrying the weight of everything, and now it feels like it's all slipping through my fingers."

"You've been carrying too much," Olivia said softly. "You can't do it all on your own. You never could. You've got to trust the people around you, Alex. You've got to trust yourself again."

Alex looked up at her, his eyes dark with the weight of his doubts. "And what if I can't? What if I've lost everything—everyone—because of my mistakes?"

Olivia leaned forward slightly, her eyes locking with his. "What if you've lost nothing? What if this is the beginning of something new? It's not too late, Alex. You still have a chance to make things right."

The words felt like a lifeline, but Alex wasn't sure if he could grab onto it. There was a part of him that was afraid—afraid that he wasn't capable of redemption, that he was too far gone to fix what he had broken.

"I don't even know where to start," Alex admitted, his voice raw. "How do I fix this? How do I fix the damage I've done to the company, to the people I've hurt?"

Olivia's expression softened, her gaze compassionate. "You start by trusting the people who have stood by you. You start by trusting Emily."

At the mention of Emily's name, Alex's heart twisted in his chest. He had thought he could let her go, that he could walk away from the pain and the betrayal. But the truth was, he couldn't. Not yet. The love he had for her—despite everything—still burned inside him, a fire he couldn't extinguish.

"I don't know if she'll ever forgive me," Alex whispered. "I don't know if I can forgive myself."

"You can't move forward if you're still holding on to the past," Olivia said gently. "You can't heal if you don't give yourself the chance to. And you can't fix the things you've broken if you're too afraid to face them."

Alex closed his eyes, the weight of her words settling over him. He didn't know if he was strong enough to face the consequences of his actions, to rebuild what had been torn apart. But he knew one thing for sure—he couldn't keep running from it. He couldn't keep hiding from the truth.

"I'll do whatever it takes," Alex said, his voice steady now, the resolve in his words clear. "But I need her. I need Emily. I need her to know that I'm trying. I need her to see that I'm not the man I was."

Olivia nodded, her expression softening. "Then go to her. Talk to her. Tell her the truth. Let her see that you're ready to be the man she deserves. But you have to do it for you, not just for her. You have to believe that you're worth the chance to redeem yourself."

Alex stood up, the weight of her words settling deep within him. He didn't have all the answers, and he didn't know what the future would hold. But for the first time in a long while, he felt a glimmer of hope. Maybe redemption wasn't impossible. Maybe, just maybe, he could find a way to fix the things that had been broken.

"I'm going to see her," Alex said, his voice resolute. "I'm going to tell her the truth. I'm going to show her that I'm not the man I was."

Olivia gave him a small, knowing smile. "You'll find your way, Alex. But it's not going to be easy. And it's not going to happen overnight."

"I know," Alex replied. "But I have to try."

As he left the office and stepped into the cold air outside, the city around him seemed to hold its breath. The road ahead was uncertain, but for the first time in what felt like forever, Alex felt like he was on the right path. He didn't know what the future held, but he knew one thing: redemption wasn't a destination. It was a journey. And the first step was finally facing the woman he loved.

The cost of truth had been steep, but Alex was ready to pay it. He was ready to prove to Emily—and to himself—that he was worth the fight.

Thirteen

The Final Choice

The rain had begun to fall softly, coating the streets of the city in a sheen of water that reflected the dim glow of the streetlights. Alex Garrett stood at the entrance of the café, his eyes tracing the droplets running down the glass as if trying to find a way to wash away the tension that had been building in his chest for days. He had come here, to this very spot, countless times before. It had been a place of solace, a place where he had found a sense of peace amidst the chaos that had defined his life. But now, it felt different. The walls seemed to close in on him, and the weight of what he was about to do pressed heavily on his shoulders.

He had made up his mind. He had chosen the path forward, no matter how painful it would be. Emily had been everything he had ever wanted and more. She had shown him what it meant to be vulnerable, to trust again, and to love without reservation.

The Final Choice

But the truth—her truth—had shattered everything. It had left him questioning who she really was, who he was, and whether they could ever rebuild what they had lost. But now, standing in the doorway of the café, he knew there was only one thing left to do: face the consequences of his choices and take the final step.

Taking a deep breath, Alex pushed open the door, the familiar chime of the bell above it sounding like a distant memory. The scent of freshly brewed coffee filled the air, but it did little to ease the nervous tightness in his chest. His eyes scanned the room, and there, in the far corner, he saw her. Emily. She was sitting alone, her hands wrapped around a steaming mug, her gaze distant, lost in thought. She looked beautiful, as always, but there was an unfamiliar sadness in her expression—something he couldn't quite place, something he had never seen before.

He hesitated for a moment, watching her from afar, and for a brief moment, he considered walking away. Maybe it would be easier. Maybe it would be less painful to let her go, to leave everything behind. But he knew that wasn't the right choice. Not anymore. He had spent so long hiding from the truth, from the consequences of his own actions, but now, there was no escaping it.

With a final exhale, Alex made his way toward the table, each step feeling heavier than the last. He reached her side, his heart pounding in his chest. Emily looked up slowly, her eyes meeting his. For a moment, neither of them spoke. The silence between them felt like a physical barrier, something they couldn't seem to cross. But then, she spoke, her voice soft, hesitant.

"Alex," she said, her eyes searching his face for something—an answer, maybe, or an explanation. "I didn't think you would come."

"I had to," Alex replied, his voice hoarse. He didn't know what to say, didn't know how to start, but the words that followed felt as though they were ripping themselves from the depths of his soul. "I had to come and see you, to tell you what's been on my mind."

Emily took a deep breath, her gaze not leaving his. "I don't know if I'm ready for this," she whispered. "I don't know if I'm ready to hear what you have to say."

Alex could see the walls she had built around herself. The distance between them had grown so vast, so unbridgeable, that he wasn't sure how to begin tearing them down. But he couldn't stop now. He had to try.

"I've made so many mistakes, Emily," he said, his voice cracking. "I've hurt you in ways I can't take back. And I don't expect you to forgive me, but I need you to understand something." He leaned in closer, his hands trembling as he placed them on the table between them. "I love you. I love you more than I've ever loved anyone. And I can't walk away from that. I can't walk away from you."

For a moment, Emily didn't move. She didn't speak. She just stared at him, her eyes searching his face as if trying to decipher the truth of his words. The silence between them stretched long, taut like a string pulled too tight. Alex could feel the weight of it pressing in on him, threatening to suffocate him, but he refused to look away. This was the moment. This was the choice.

"I don't know how to trust you anymore," Emily said quietly, her voice breaking the silence. "I don't know if I can ever trust you again. You kept so many things from me, Alex. You kept everything from me. And the truth… the truth changed everything."

Alex felt the sting of her words, but he didn't flinch. He knew she was right. He had lied to her. He had kept secrets from her that had torn their relationship apart. But now, standing before her, he realized that those lies were not the full story. They were just pieces of a much bigger picture—a picture that had to be painted with truth, no matter how painful.

"I never wanted to hurt you, Emily," he said, his voice rough with emotion. "I thought I was protecting you by keeping things from you, by keeping my past buried. But now, I see that it was just another way to keep us apart. I'm sorry for everything I've done. I'm sorry for making you doubt me. But I can't change the past. All I can do is ask for your forgiveness."

Emily's eyes shimmered with unshed tears, but she didn't let them fall. She sat back in her chair, her arms folded across her chest, as if trying to protect herself from what he was saying. Her face was a mixture of pain, confusion, and something else— something that Alex couldn't quite name.

"I don't know what to do, Alex," she said, her voice barely above a whisper. "I don't know if I can forgive you. I don't know if I can ever look at you the same way again."

Alex's heart sank at her words, but he didn't back down. He couldn't. "I don't expect you to forgive me right away," he said. "But I need you to know that I'm here. I'm not going anywhere. And I'm willing to do whatever it takes to prove to you that I'm not the man I was. I'm willing to fight for you. If you'll let me."

For a long moment, Emily didn't speak. She just sat there, her gaze locked on his, as if weighing his words, searching for the truth beneath them. Alex held his breath, the air thick with anticipation, with the uncertainty of what was to come. He had laid himself bare before her. He had told her everything—everything that had been eating away at him for months. And now, it was up to her.

"I don't know, Alex," Emily finally said, her voice fragile. "I don't know if I can believe you anymore. I don't know if I can trust you the way I did before. You hurt me. You lied to me. And that changes things."

Alex felt a sharp pain in his chest, but he didn't look away. He had to hear this. He had to know if there was any chance, any possibility, of redemption.

"I know I hurt you," he said softly. "But I want you to know that I never wanted to. I never meant to cause you pain. I was afraid. I was afraid of losing you, and I thought that if I kept my past hidden, I could protect you from it. But now I see how wrong I was."

The Final Choice

Emily blinked, and for a moment, the vulnerability in her eyes mirrored the same fear Alex had felt for so long. Fear of rejection, fear of facing the truth. Fear of facing the consequences of their actions.

"I don't know what the future holds, Alex," she said, her voice shaky. "But I can't ignore the past. And I can't ignore what I feel right now. I need time. I need to figure out if this is something worth fighting for."

Alex nodded slowly, his heart heavy with the weight of her words. "I understand," he said quietly. "Take all the time you need. I won't push you. But I'll be here. When you're ready, I'll be here."

Emily looked up at him, her eyes filled with uncertainty and a quiet sadness. "I don't know if I'll ever be ready," she whispered.

Alex stood up slowly, the ache in his chest deepening. He had hoped that this moment would be different—that he would walk away knowing whether they had a future together or not. But instead, all he had was this—an unanswered question, an uncertain future, and the knowledge that he had done everything he could.

"I'll be waiting," he said softly. "Whenever you're ready."

And with that, he turned and walked out of the café, leaving Emily behind. The rain had picked up now, the drops hitting the pavement with a steady rhythm. But as Alex walked into the storm, he knew that this was only the beginning. The final choice had been made. And now, all that was left was to wait.

Fourteen

The Heart's Desire

The storm outside raged with a ferocity that matched Alex Garrett's turbulent emotions. Rain lashed against the windows of his apartment, and the occasional flash of lightning illuminated the darkened room. Alex sat on the edge of his bed, his head bowed, his hands clasped together as though in prayer. The silence within him was deafening, broken only by the rhythmic pounding of rain on glass.

It had been weeks since his conversation with Emily. Weeks of waiting, hoping, and agonizing over whether she would find it in her heart to forgive him. Every passing day felt like a lifetime, and every time his phone buzzed, he felt his heart leap in anticipation—only to sink again when it wasn't her.

He had poured his soul out to her, confessed his love and his regret, but her hesitation had been clear. She was still deciding, still weighing the cost of trusting him again. And Alex didn't blame her. He had given her every reason to doubt him, every reason to walk away. But that didn't stop him from longing for her, from dreaming of a future where they could move past the lies and start anew.

The city outside was a blur of lights and shadows, the storm casting an ethereal glow over the skyline. Alex stood and moved to the window, placing a hand against the cool glass. His reflection stared back at him, a man transformed by pain, loss, and love. He had spent so much of his life chasing things that didn't matter—money, power, prestige—only to realize too late that none of it could fill the void inside him. Emily had shown him what truly mattered, and now, the thought of losing her forever was almost too much to bear.

His phone buzzed on the nightstand, jolting him from his thoughts. He turned sharply, his heart pounding as he reached for it. The screen lit up, and for a moment, he just stared at the name displayed there.

Emily.

His breath caught in his throat. His fingers trembled as he swiped to answer. He pressed the phone to his ear, his voice barely steady as he spoke.

"Emily?"

There was a pause on the other end, a silence that stretched for an eternity before her voice came through—soft, hesitant, and

The Heart's Desire

achingly familiar.

"Alex," she said. "Can we talk?"

His heart raced, a mixture of hope and dread coursing through him. "Of course," he replied, his voice steady despite the storm raging inside him. "Where are you?"

"I'm at the park," she said quietly. "The one by the river. Can you meet me here?"

"I'll be there in ten minutes," Alex said without hesitation.

The line went dead, and Alex grabbed his coat, throwing it on as he rushed out of the apartment. The rain was unrelenting, drenching him the moment he stepped outside, but he didn't care. His footsteps echoed on the slick pavement as he made his way to the park, his mind racing with thoughts of what she might say. Was she ready to forgive him? Or was this her way of saying goodbye?

The park was nearly empty when he arrived, the storm having driven most people indoors. The river churned angrily beneath the bridge, the sound of the rushing water mingling with the patter of rain. And there, standing beneath the shelter of a large oak tree, was Emily.

She wore a long coat, her hair damp and clinging to her face. She looked up as he approached, her eyes meeting his, and for a moment, the world seemed to hold its breath. Alex slowed his steps as he reached her, the space between them charged with unspoken words.

"You came," she said softly, her voice barely audible over the rain.

"Of course I did," Alex replied, his gaze never leaving hers. "I told you I'd be here whenever you were ready."

Emily looked down, her hands fidgeting with the edge of her coat. "I didn't know if you meant it," she admitted. "I didn't know if you'd wait."

"I would've waited forever," Alex said, his voice firm. "If that's what it took."

She looked up at him then, her eyes glistening with tears. "I've been thinking a lot about what you said," she began. "About everything that's happened between us. And I've been trying to figure out if I can let go of the hurt, the lies, and the betrayal."

Alex's heart clenched at her words, but he forced himself to stay silent, to let her speak.

"I kept telling myself that I couldn't trust you again," she continued, her voice trembling. "That I couldn't risk opening myself up to that kind of pain. But no matter how much I tried to convince myself, I couldn't stop thinking about you. About us."

She took a shaky breath, her hands clasping together as though trying to steady herself. "You hurt me, Alex. You broke my trust in ways I didn't think were possible. But you also showed me something I'd never felt before. You showed me what it means to love someone with your whole heart, even when it scares you."

Alex felt a lump rise in his throat, his chest tightening as he listened to her. He wanted to reach out, to hold her, but he stayed rooted in place, afraid of breaking the fragile moment between them.

"I don't know if I can forget what happened," Emily said, her voice cracking. "But I think… I think I can forgive you. I want to try. I want to believe that we can move past this, that we can build something real."

The words hit Alex like a tidal wave, a surge of relief and emotion washing over him. He stepped closer, his voice trembling as he spoke. "Emily, I promise you, I will spend every day proving that you made the right choice. I will never take your forgiveness for granted. And I will never stop trying to be the man you deserve."

A tear slipped down Emily's cheek, and she gave a small, shaky smile. "I don't need you to be perfect, Alex. I just need you to be honest. No more secrets. No more lies."

"No more lies," Alex vowed, his voice steady with conviction. "I'll give you everything I have—everything I am."

For a moment, neither of them spoke. The rain continued to fall, but it felt distant now, a mere backdrop to the moment unfolding between them. Alex reached out slowly, his hand brushing against hers, and she didn't pull away. Instead, she stepped closer, her eyes locked on his.

"I'm scared," Emily whispered, her voice barely audible. "But I want to try. I want to see if we can make this work."

Alex cupped her face gently, his thumb brushing away the tear that had fallen. "We can," he said softly. "We will. Together."

And then, as the storm raged on around them, Alex leaned in, pressing his lips to hers. The kiss was tender, filled with all the unspoken emotions that had been building between them for so long. It was a promise, a plea, and a declaration all at once. When they finally pulled apart, Emily rested her forehead against his, her eyes closed as she let out a shaky breath.

"This is what I want," she said quietly. "You're what I want."

Alex smiled, his heart swelling with a mixture of joy and relief. "And you're all I've ever wanted, Emily. My heart's desire."

As they stood there, wrapped in each other's arms, Alex felt the weight of the past begin to lift. The road ahead wouldn't be easy, but for the first time, he felt ready to face it. With Emily by his side, he knew they could weather any storm. Together, they would find a way to heal, to rebuild, and to create the life they had both been searching for.

Fifteen

A Love Rekindled

The morning sun broke through the clouds after weeks of relentless rain, casting a golden glow over the small town. It was as though nature itself had decided to gift Alex and Emily a clean slate. The air was crisp and fresh, filled with the earthy scent of wet grass and the faint hum of birdsong. Alex stood at the edge of the park by the river, the same place where Emily had given him a second chance, where she had dared to believe in him again. His heart thudded in his chest as he waited, his gaze fixed on the winding path ahead.

It had been a week since their emotional reunion in the rain—a week of cautious rebuilding, of tentative steps toward something new. They had agreed to take things slowly, to give themselves the space to heal and to rediscover the trust that had been broken. But today, Alex was determined to show her that he was ready to move forward, that he was committed to making things right.

He checked his watch for what felt like the hundredth time, his nerves getting the better of him. He had spent the last few days planning every detail of this moment, wanting it to be perfect. But now, as the seconds ticked by, doubt began to creep in. What if it was too soon? What if she wasn't ready? What if he wasn't ready?

The sound of footsteps on the gravel path pulled him from his thoughts. He turned, his breath catching in his throat as he saw Emily approaching. She wore a simple white dress that fluttered in the gentle breeze, her hair falling in loose waves around her shoulders. She looked radiant, her smile tentative but warm as their eyes met. Alex felt his heart swell, a wave of emotion crashing over him.

"Hi," Emily said softly as she reached him, her voice carrying a hint of nervousness.

"Hi," Alex replied, his own voice steady despite the storm of emotions inside him. "You look beautiful."

A faint blush crept across her cheeks, and she looked down, tucking a strand of hair behind her ear. "Thank you. You look… nervous."

Alex let out a small laugh, rubbing the back of his neck. "I guess I am," he admitted. "I just want today to go well."

Emily tilted her head, her smile growing. "It's already going

A Love Rekindled

well. You're here. I'm here. That's enough, isn't it?"

Her words were simple, but they carried a weight that Alex felt deep in his chest. She was right. They didn't need grand gestures or perfect plans. They just needed each other.

"Come with me," Alex said, extending his hand.

Emily hesitated for a moment before placing her hand in his. The warmth of her touch sent a spark through him, and he gave her fingers a gentle squeeze. Together, they walked down the path that wound along the riverbank, the sunlight dancing on the water's surface. The silence between them was comfortable, the kind of silence that spoke of understanding and connection.

As they rounded a bend, Emily stopped, her eyes widening at the sight before her. A small wooden dock extended out over the river, decorated with string lights that twinkled in the sunlight. A picnic blanket was spread out at the end of the dock, laden with an assortment of food and a bottle of wine. A bouquet of wildflowers sat in a small vase, their vibrant colors a stark contrast to the calm blue of the river.

"Alex..." Emily whispered, her voice filled with awe. "Did you do all this?"

Alex smiled, his heart pounding. "I wanted to do something special for you. For us. I thought... maybe we could start fresh."

Emily turned to him, her eyes glistening. "You didn't have to do all this. You know that, right?"

"I know," Alex said, his voice soft. "But I wanted to. I wanted to show you how much you mean to me."

Emily's gaze lingered on him for a moment before she stepped closer, wrapping her arms around his waist. Alex froze for a moment, the unexpected intimacy catching him off guard, but then he relaxed, his arms encircling her. He held her tightly, his heart aching with gratitude and love.

"Thank you," she murmured against his chest. "This is… perfect."

They sat down on the dock, the sunlight warming their skin as they shared the meal Alex had prepared. The conversation flowed easily, the tension that had once lingered between them replaced by a newfound sense of ease. They laughed, reminisced, and talked about the future—about what they wanted, what they hoped for, and what they were willing to fight for.

As the afternoon wore on, the sun dipped lower in the sky, casting a golden hue over the river. Alex leaned back on his hands, his gaze fixed on Emily as she spoke. He found himself mesmerized by the way the light caught in her hair, the way her eyes sparkled when she laughed. He had never felt this way before—so completely and utterly at peace.

"Emily," Alex said, his voice cutting through the gentle hum of the river. She turned to him, her expression curious. "There's something I need to say."

Her smile faltered slightly, and she straightened, giving him her full attention. "What is it?"

Alex took a deep breath, his heart hammering in his chest. "I know I've said this before, but I need you to hear it again. I love you. I've loved you from the moment I met you, even when I didn't know how to show it. And I know I've made mistakes—mistakes that hurt you, that made you question everything about us. But I want you to know that I'm here. I'm not going anywhere. And I'll spend the rest of my life proving to you that I'm worth the chance you're giving me."

Emily's eyes filled with tears, but she didn't look away. She reached out, placing her hand over his. "Alex, I know you mean every word of that. And I believe you. But it's not just about proving yourself to me. It's about us—about both of us being willing to fight for this, to fight for each other."

"I am," Alex said, his voice firm. "I'll fight for us, Emily. I'll fight for you."

A single tear slipped down her cheek, and she smiled—a smile so radiant it took his breath away. "Then let's do this," she said softly. "Let's stop looking back. Let's build something new. Together."

Alex felt a surge of emotion so powerful it threatened to overwhelm him. He reached out, cupping her face in his hands, and kissed her. The world seemed to fade away in that moment, leaving only the two of them, their love rekindled, their hearts beating as one.

When they finally pulled apart, Emily rested her forehead against his, her eyes closed, her smile still lingering. "I love you, Alex," she whispered. "I always have."

"And I love you," Alex replied, his voice steady. "Forever."

The sun dipped below the horizon, painting the sky in shades of pink and gold. As the first stars began to appear, Alex and Emily sat together on the dock, their hands intertwined, their hearts full. The journey they had been on had been long and painful, but it had brought them to this moment—a moment of hope, of healing, and of love rekindled. And as they looked out over the river, they knew that, together, they could face whatever the future held.

www.ingramcontent.com/pod-product-compliance
Lightning Source LLC
LaVergne TN
LVHW020423080526
838202LV00055B/5011